BRANDON HEATH
WHAT IF WE

PIANO
VOCAL
GUITAR

D0504052

ISBN 978-1-4234-9456-0

HAL•LEONARD® CORPORATION
7777 W. BLUEMOUND RD. P.O. BOX 13819 MILWAUKEE, WI 53213

Visit Hal Leonard Online at
www.halleonard.com

5   GIVE ME YOUR EYES

12   WAIT AND SEE

16   TRUST YOU

22   LONDON

28   SUNRISE

33   SORE EYES

38   LOVE NEVER FAILS

43   LISTEN UP

48   FIGHT ANOTHER DAY

54   WHEN I'M ALONE

58   NO NOT ONE

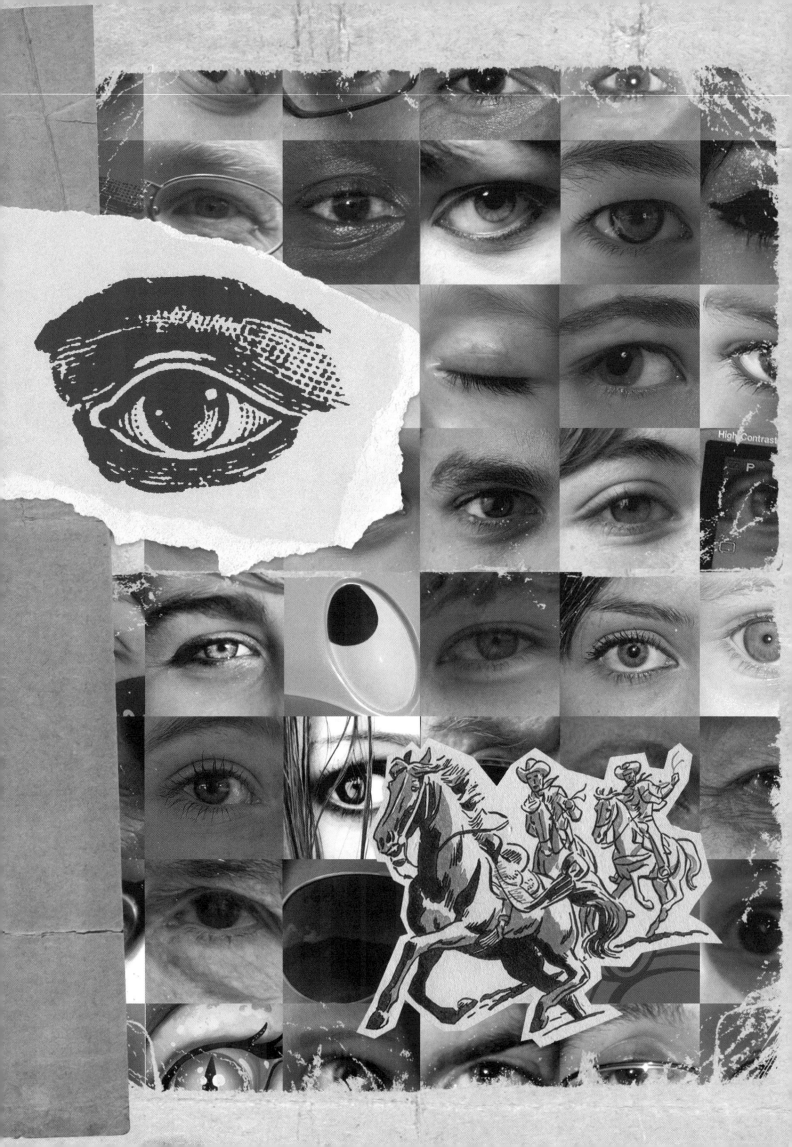

GIVE ME YOUR EYES

Words and Music by JASON INGRAM
and BRANDON HEATH

* Recorded a half step lower.

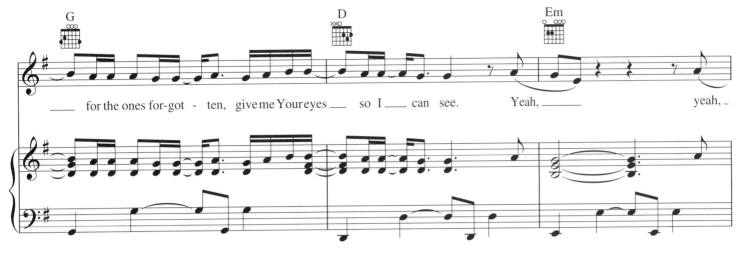

for the ones for-got - ten, give me Your eyes __ so I __ can see. Yeah, _____ yeah, _

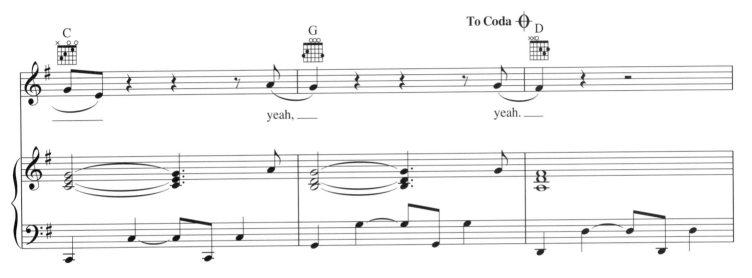

To Coda

yeah, ___ yeah. ___

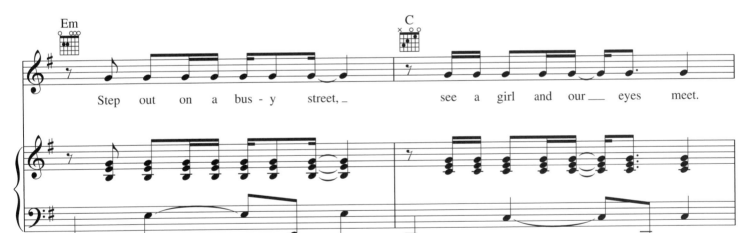

Step out on a bus-y street, _ see a girl and our __ eyes meet.

Does her best to smile _ at me _ to hide what's un - der - neath. _

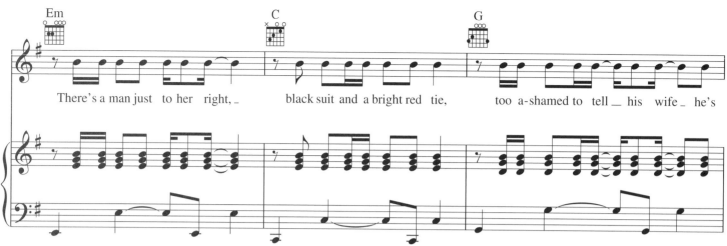

There's a man just to her right, _ black suit and a bright red tie, too a-shamed to tell _ his wife _ he's

out of work; _ he's buy-ing time. _ All those peo - ple go - ing some - where. Why _

_ have I _ nev - er _ cared? Give me Your eyes _

D.S. al Coda

CODA

I've been here a mil - lion times; a cou - ple of mil - lion eyes

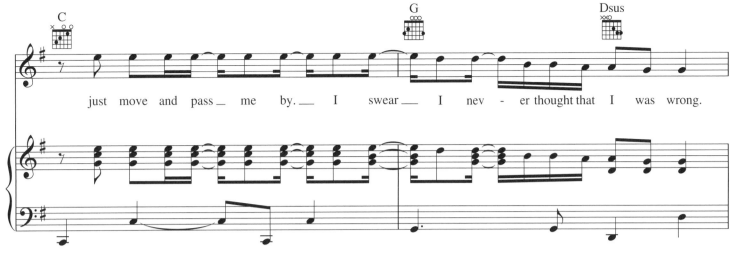

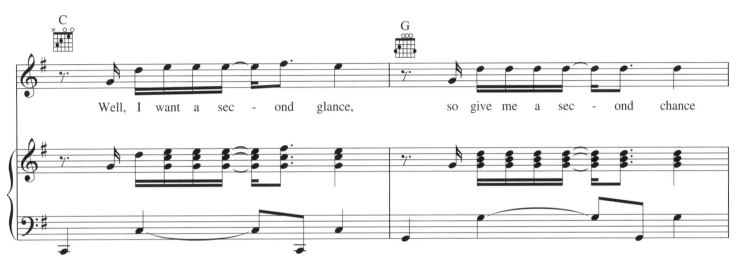

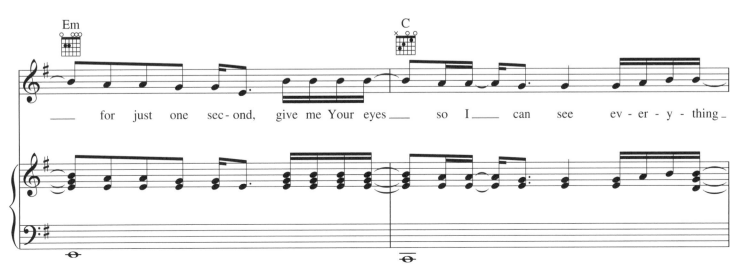

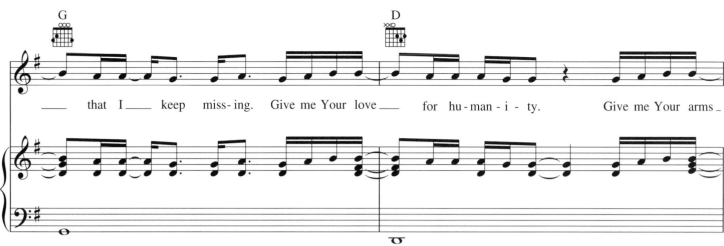

____ that I ____ keep miss- ing. Give me Your love ____ for hu - man - i - ty. Give me Your arms _

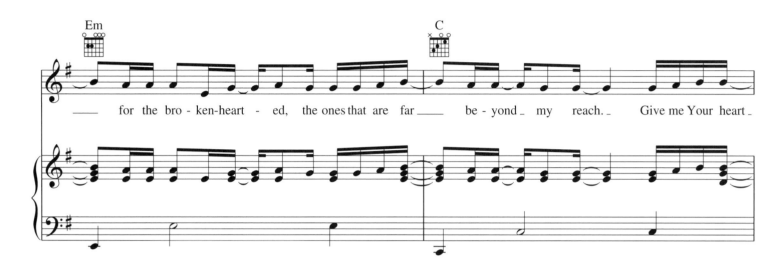

____ for the bro - ken-heart - ed, the ones that are far ____ be - yond _ my reach. ____ Give me Your heart _

____ for the ones for - got - ten, give me Your eyes ____ so I ____ can see. Give me Your eyes _

(Lead vocal ad lib.)

____ for just one sec - ond, give me Your eyes ____ so I ____ can see ev - er - y - thing _

that I __ keep miss-ing. Give me Your love __ for hu-man-i-ty. Give me Your arms __

for the bro-ken-heart-ed, the ones that are far __ be-yond __ my reach. __ Give me Your heart __

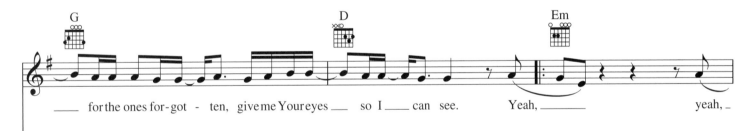

for the ones for-got-ten, give me Your eyes __ so I __ can see. Yeah, _____ yeah, __

yeah, ___   yeah. ___   Yeah, __ __

WAIT AND SEE

Words and Music by
BRANDON HEATH

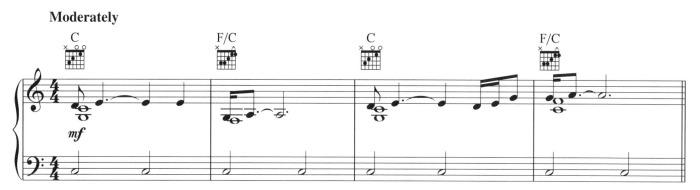

I was born in Ten-nes-see, _____ late Ju-ly hu-mid-i-ty. _____
nev-er real-ly was that good in school. _____ I talked too much, broke the rules.
now's my time to be a man, _____ fol-low my heart as far as I can.

Doc-tor said I was luck-y to be a-live. _____ I've been
Teach-ers thought I was a hope-less fool, al-right.   I
No tell-ing where I'm end-ing up _____ to-night. _____   I

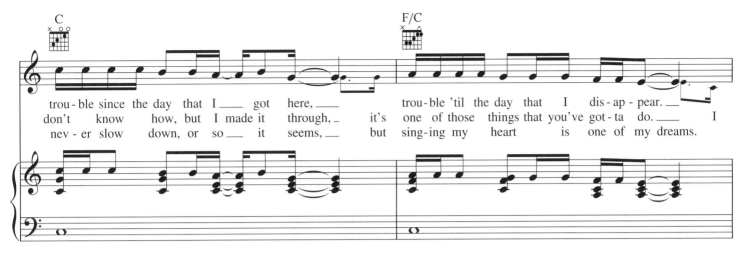

trou-ble since the day that I ___ got here, ___ trou-ble 'til the day that I dis-ap-pear. ___
don't know how, but I made it through, ___ it's one of those things that you've got-ta do. ___ I
nev-er slow down, or so ___ it seems, ___ but sing-ing my heart is one of my dreams.

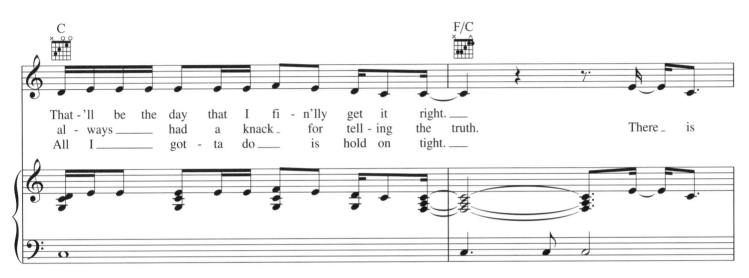

That-'ll be the day that I fi-n'lly get it right. ___
al-ways ___ had a knack ___ for tell-ing the truth.
All I ___ got-ta do ___ is hold on tight. ___

There ___ is

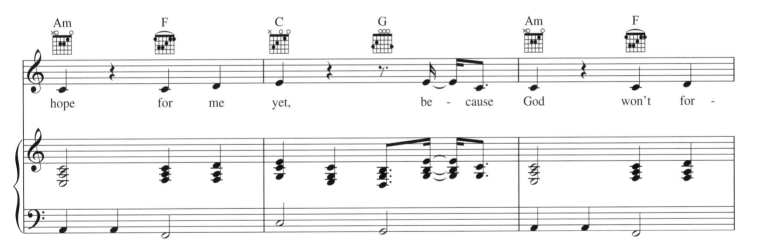

hope for me yet, be - cause God won't for -

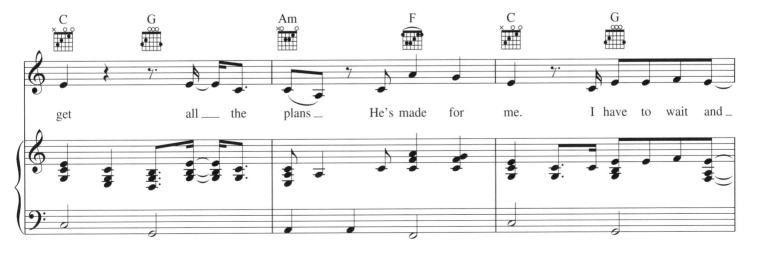

get all ___ the plans ___ He's made for me. I have to wait and ___

see. ___ He's not fin-ished with ___ me yet.

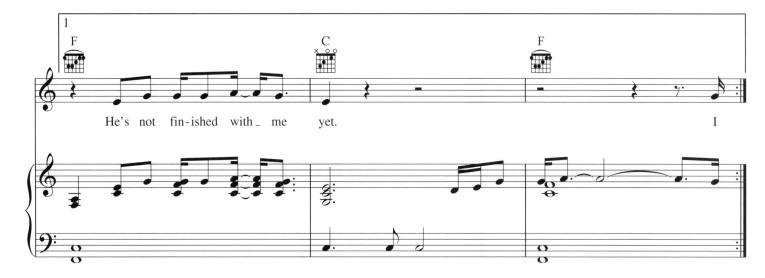

1

He's not fin-ished with ___ me yet. I

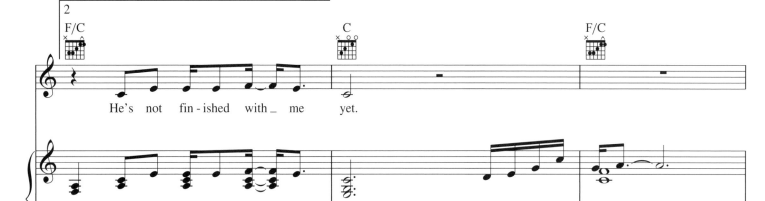

2

He's not fin-ished with ___ me yet.

Still won-der-ing why I'm here, still wres-tl-ing with my fear, but oh, _____ He's up to

some - thing.

And the far - ther on I go, I've seen e - nough to know that

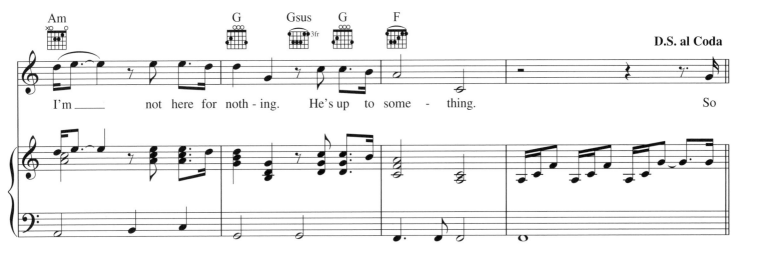

D.S. al Coda

I'm ___ not here for noth - ing. He's up to some - thing. So

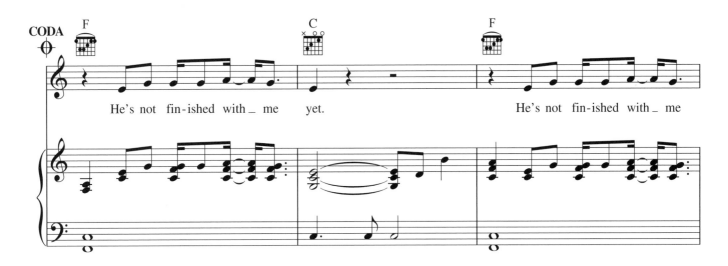

CODA

He's not fin-ished with ___ me yet.

He's not fin-ished with ___ me

yet.

He's not fin-ished with ___ me yet.

TRUST YOU

Words and Music by JASON INGRAM
and BRANDON HEATH

I can't walk _ with-out _ watch-ing where _ I'm go - ing.

I can't speak _ with-out _ know-ing what to say. _

I can't love _ and have _ an-y hes-i-ta - tion, 'cause I

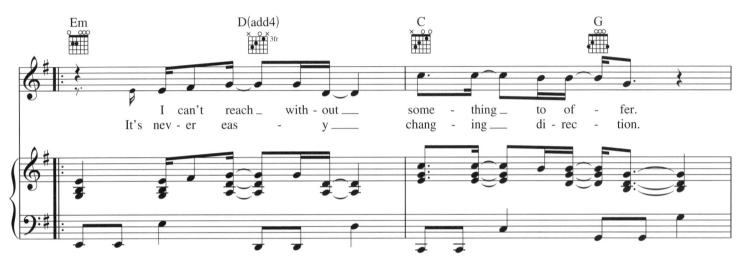

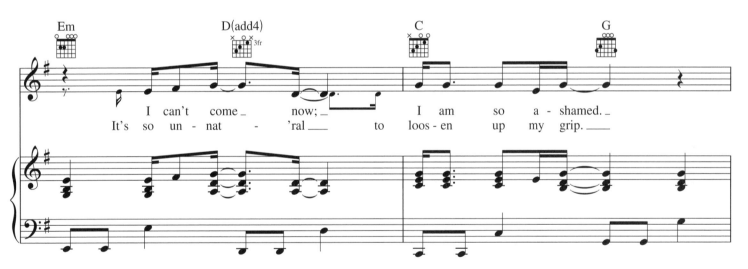

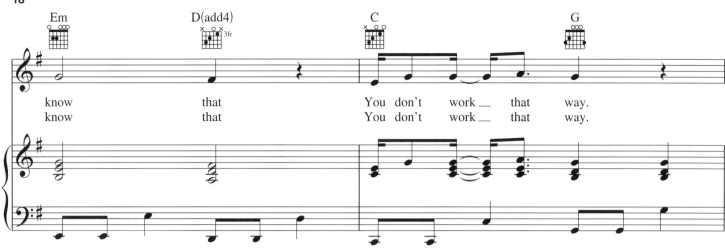

know   that   You don't work __ that   way.
know   that   You don't work __ that   way.

I'm not gon - na fight __ You an - y - more. ____

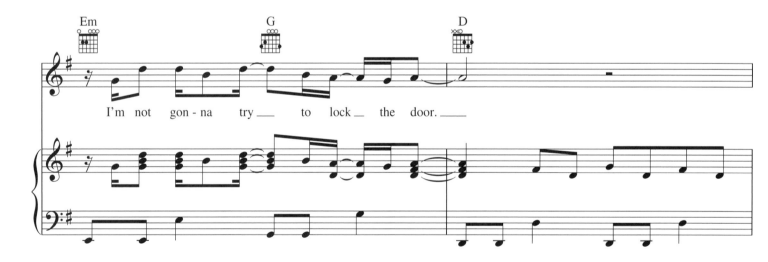

I'm not gon - na try __ to lock __ the door. ____

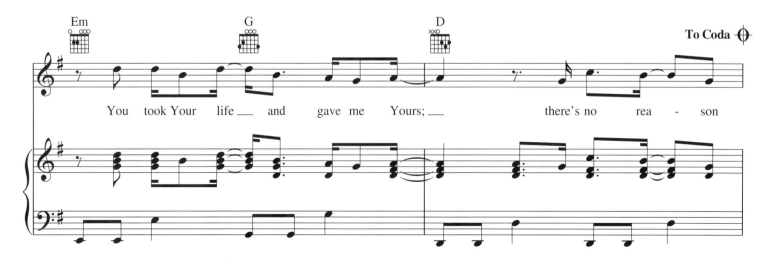

You took Your life __ and gave me Yours; __ there's no rea - son

I must now sur - ren - der. There's no oth - er way.

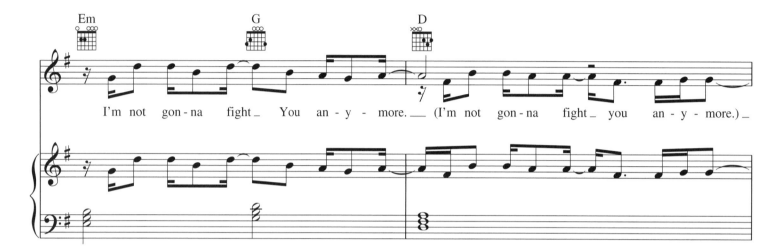

I'm not gon - na fight __ You an - y - more. __ (I'm not gon - na fight __ you an - y - more.) __

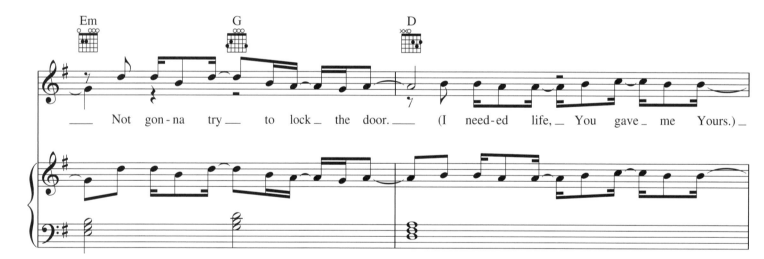

__ Not gon - na try __ to lock __ the door. __ (I need - ed life, __ You gave __ me Yours.) __

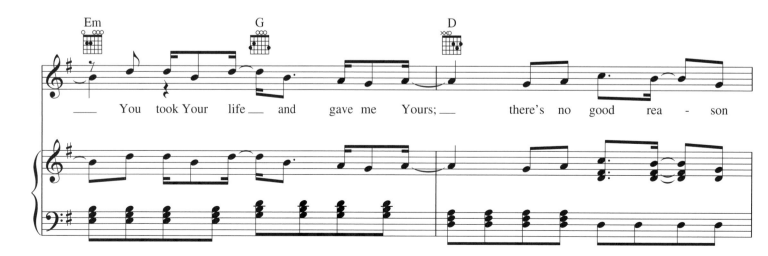

__ You took Your life __ and gave me Yours; __ there's no good rea - son

D.S. al Coda

why

I should-n't trust __ You.

CODA

why,

no good rea - son why

I should - n't trust __ You

with mine.

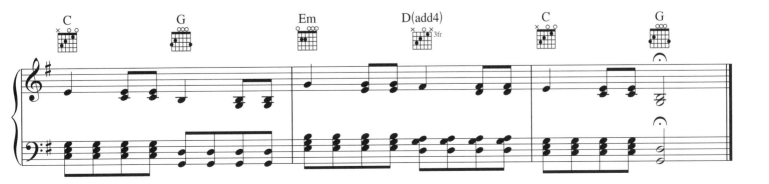

LONDON

Words and Music by BRANDON HEATH
and CHAD CATES

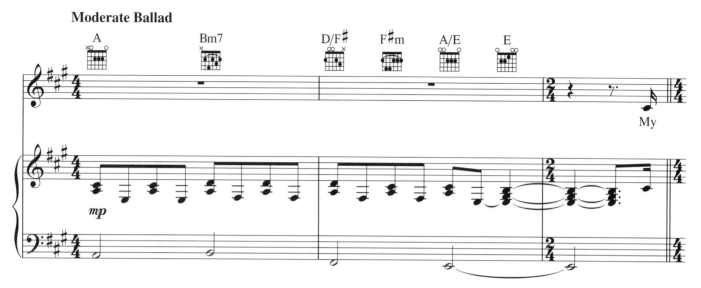

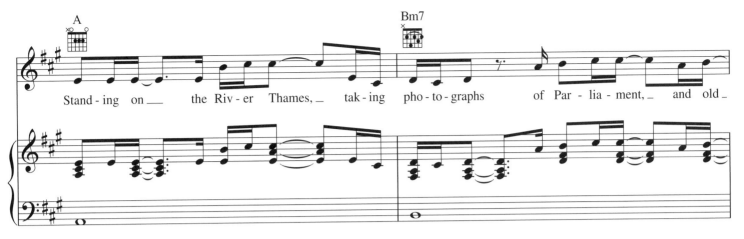

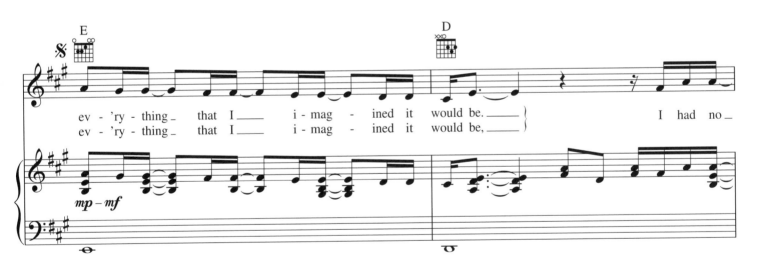

to - night _____ while I _____ stand here and cry, _____ watch-ing

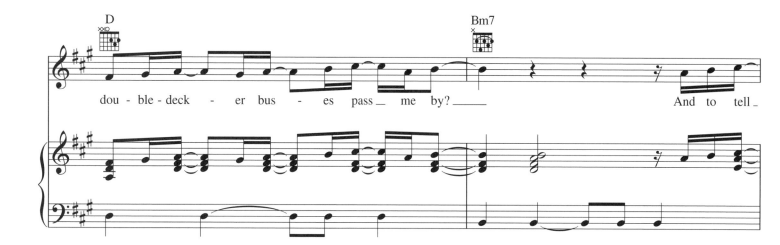

dou - ble-deck - er bus - es pass _ me by? _____ And to tell _

_ you the truth, _ it's all _____ that I _ can do _____ to keep from

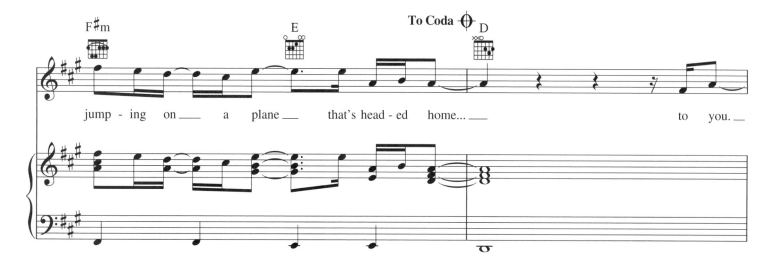

jump-ing on _ a plane _ that's head-ed home... _ to you. _

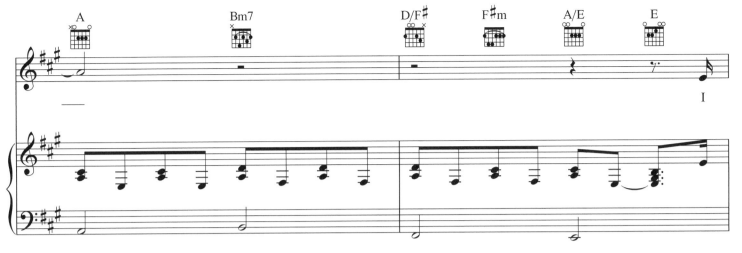

took a stroll ___ down Ab - bey Road, ___ tried to peek in - side the stu - di - os, and

some - where 'long ___ the way, ___ I bought you flow - ers and a

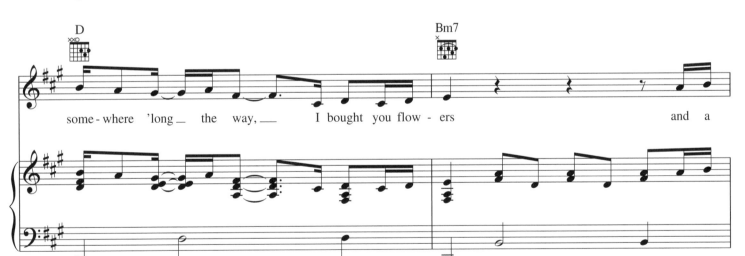

pock - et map ___ of the Un - der - ground ___ 'cause you and I both know ___ I get turned a - round. ___ I'm so ___

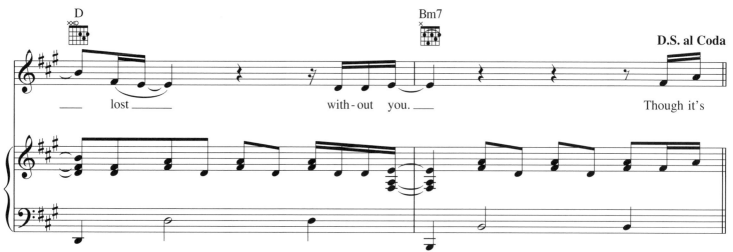

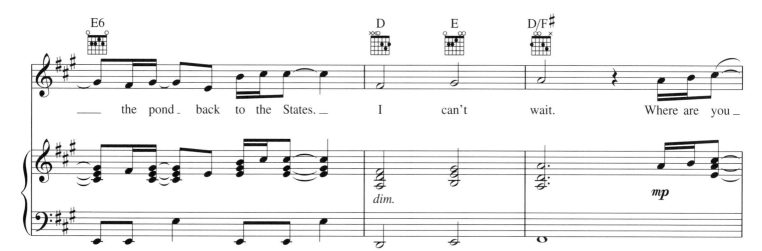

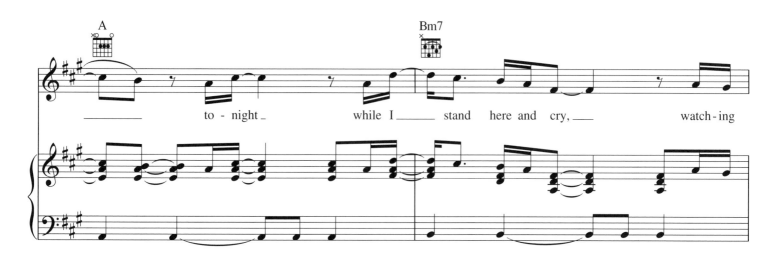

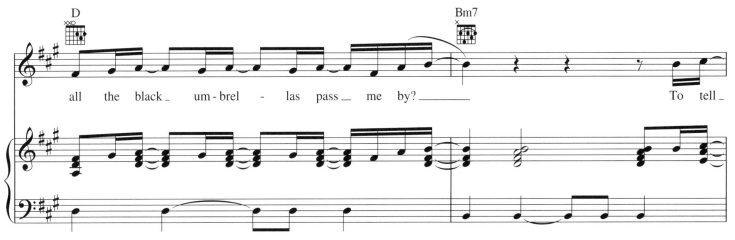

all the black_ um - brel - las pass_ me by?_____ To tell_

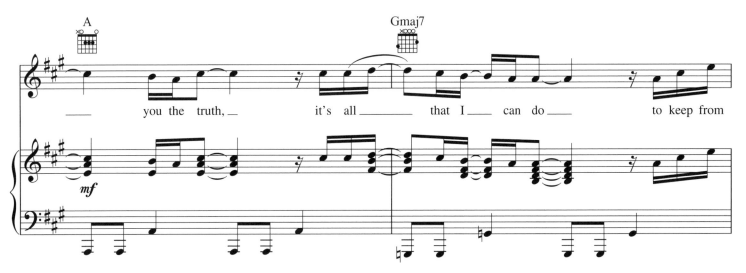

____ you the truth, __ it's all _____ that I __ can do ____ to keep from

jump - ing on __ a plane __ that's head-ed home, ___ so I'm

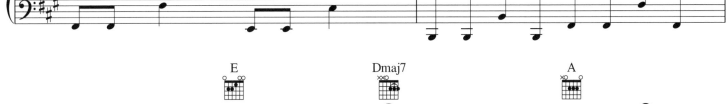

jump - ing on __ a plane __ head-ed home __ to you. ___

SUNRISE

Words and Music by BRANDON HEATH,
DANIEL MUCKALA and NATE CAMPANY

Moderately fast

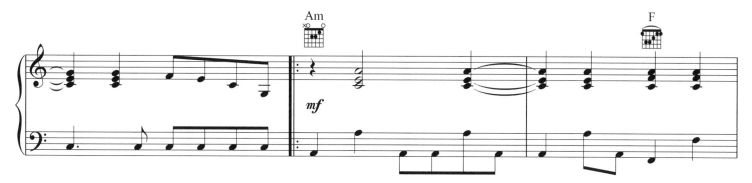

You wan - na sound off, but you can't find the words to. _____

Hold - ing your days like a stack of _____ pa - per, _____ then you're

Recorded a half step lower.

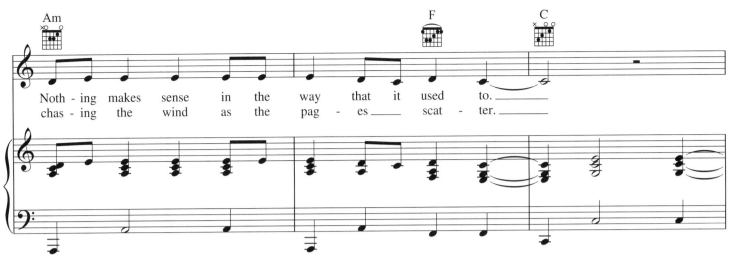

Noth - ing makes sense in the way that it used to. _____
chas - ing the wind as the pag - es _____ scat - ter. _____

You can save a _____ few, but you can't get them all back. _____
Can't find the plus in the pos - i - tive think - ing. _____

The well's _____ run dry and you're
So get _____ out fast with your

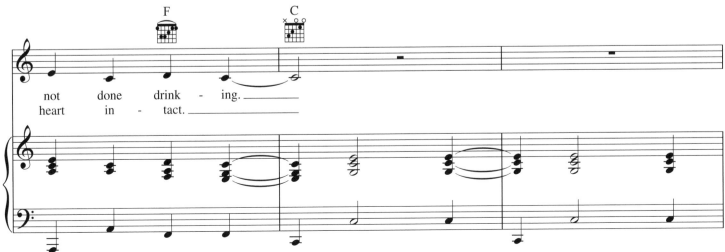

not done drink - ing. _____
heart in - tact. _____

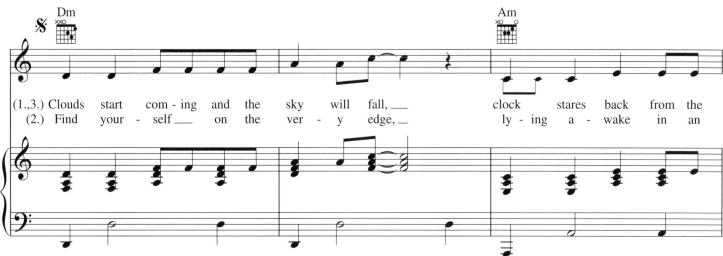

(1.,3.) Clouds start com-ing and the sky will fall, ___ clock stares back from the
(2.) Find your-self ___ on the ver - y edge, ___ ly-ing a-wake in an

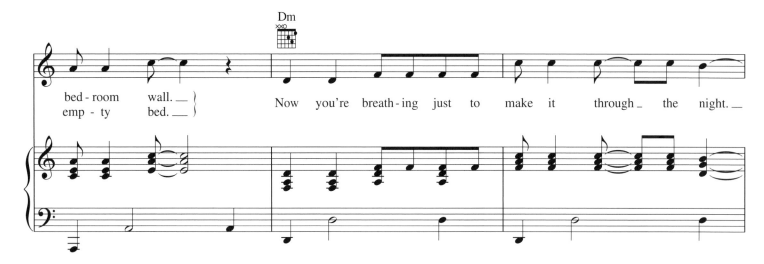

bed - room wall. ___ }
emp - ty bed. ___ }
Now you're breath-ing just to make it through ___ the night. ___

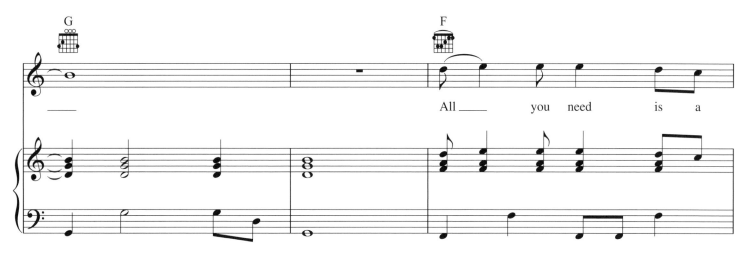

___ All ___ you need is a

sun - rise, just a mo - ment of dawn.

If _____ you're lost in the twi - light, close _ your eyes and move

on. When _ you're tired in the wait - ing,

e - ven though _____ it's gon - na take you a lit - tle more time, _____

_____ just a lit - tle more time, the sun's gon - na find _ you. _

SORE EYES

Words and Music by BRANDON HEATH,
DAN HASELTINE, CHARLIE LOWELL,
STEPHEN MASON and MATT ODMARK

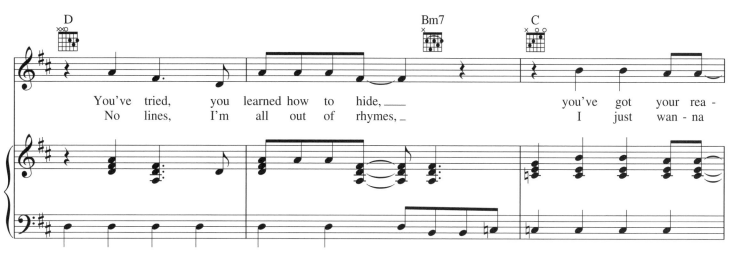

- sons. _____ I bet you're full of re- gret, ___ sweet
hold you. _____ I bet I'll make you for- get, ___ love's

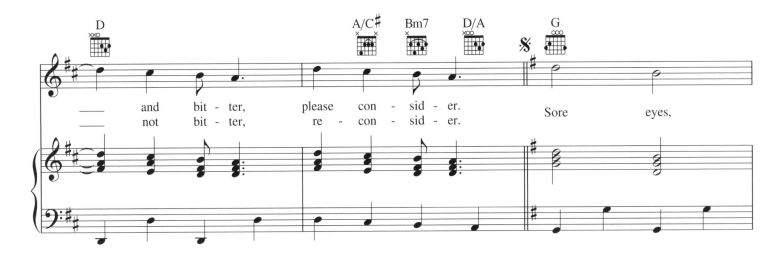

___ and bit - ter, please con - sid - er.
___ not bit - ter, re - con - sid - er. Sore eyes,

what's up with that face? ___ Think we can trace ___ these lines ___

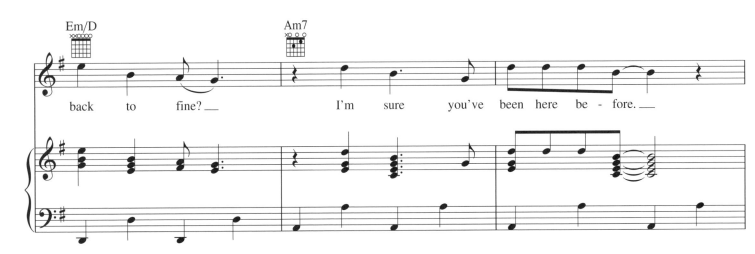

back to fine? ___ I'm sure you've been here be - fore. ___

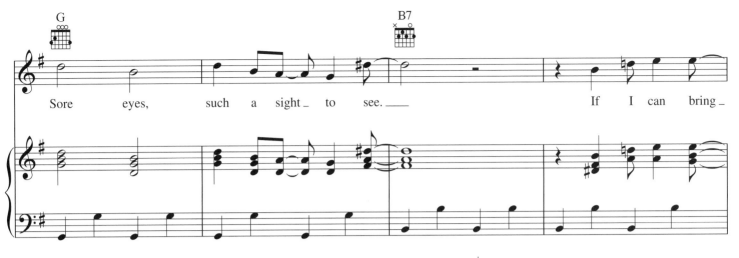

Sore eyes, such a sight to see. If I can bring

that light back to your eyes to stay, what would you say, what would you say?

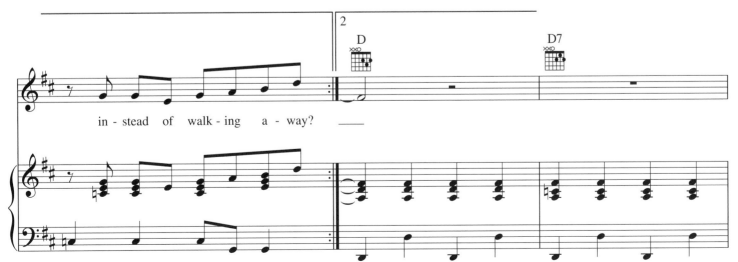

in-stead of walk-ing a-way?

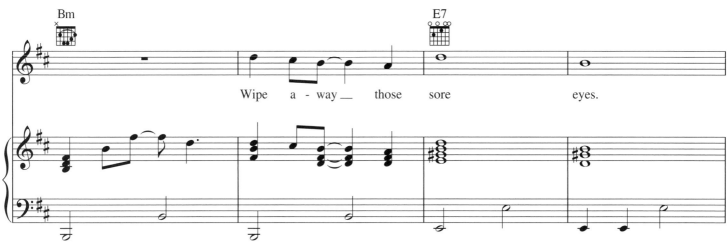

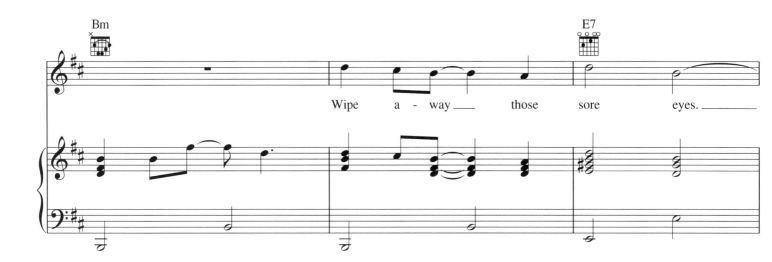

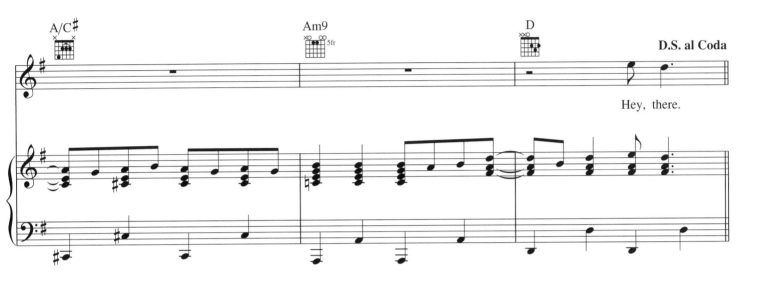

Hey, there.

what would you say? _____ What would you say? _

What would you say? ___ Whad-da-ya say?

LOVE NEVER FAILS

Words and Music by BRANDON HEATH
and CHAD CATES

Love is not proud,
Love will sus - tain,

love does not boast, love, af - ter all, mat - ters ___ the
love will pro - vide, love will not cease at the end ___ of _____

most. Love does not run,
time. Love will pro - tect,

love does not ___ hide, love does not keep locked in - side.
love al - ways ___ hopes, love still be - lieves when you ___ don't.

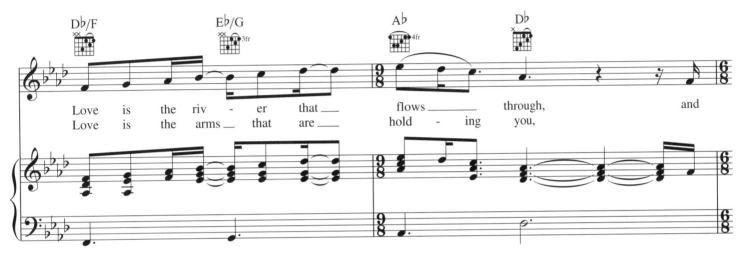

Love is the riv - er that ___ flows ___ through, and
Love is the arms ___ that are ___ hold - ing you,

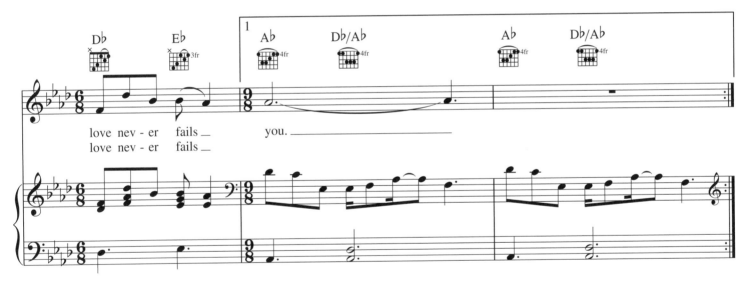

love nev - er fails ___ you. ___
love nev - er fails ___

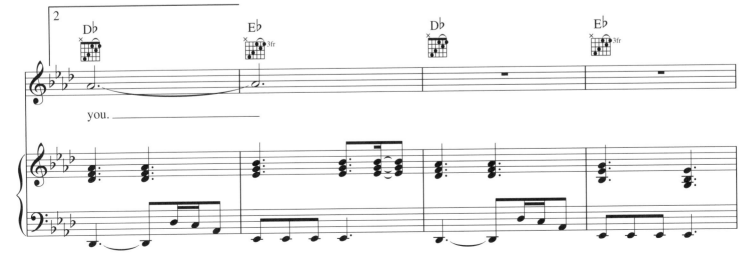

you. ___

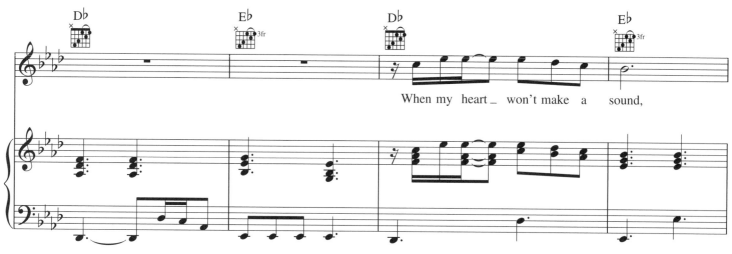

When my heart __ won't make a sound,

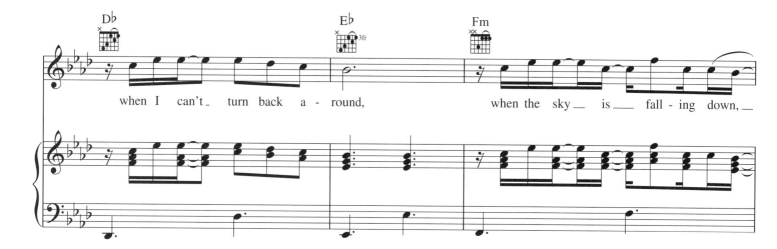

when I can't __ turn back a - round, when the sky __ is __ fall - ing down, __

__ noth - ing is __ great - er than this, __ great - er than this. __

'Cause love is right here, love is a - live,

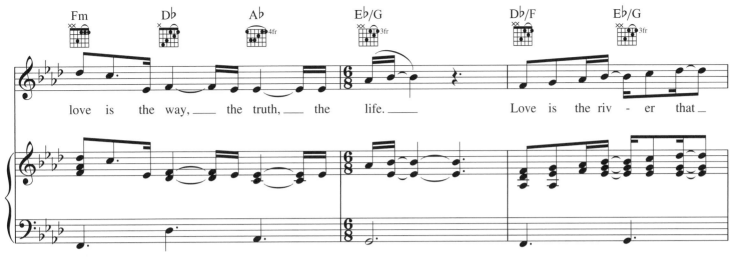

love is the way, ____ the truth, ___ the life. ____ Love is the riv - er that _

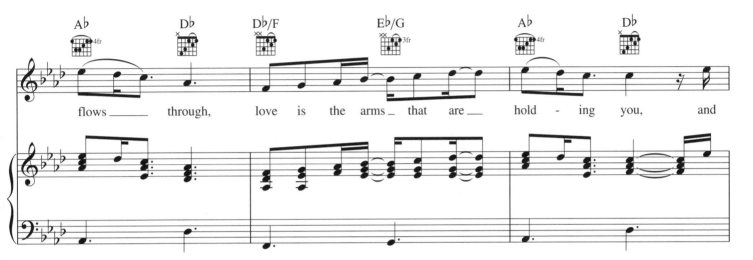

flows _____ through, love is the arms _ that are ___ hold - ing you, and

love is the place _ you will fly _____ to. Love nev - er fails __

you.

LISTEN UP

Words and Music by JASON INGRAM
and BRANDON HEATH

Moderately slow, in 2

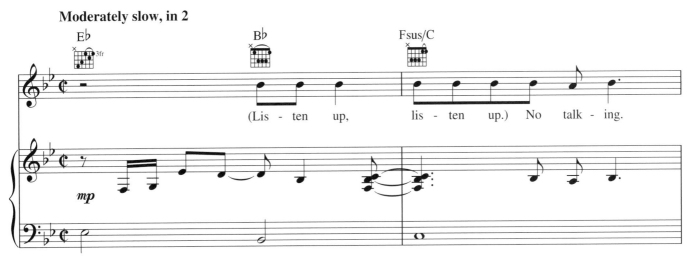

(Lis - ten up, lis - ten up.) No talk - ing.

(Lis - ten up, lis - ten up.) I'm lis - t'ning now. _____ (Lis - ten up,

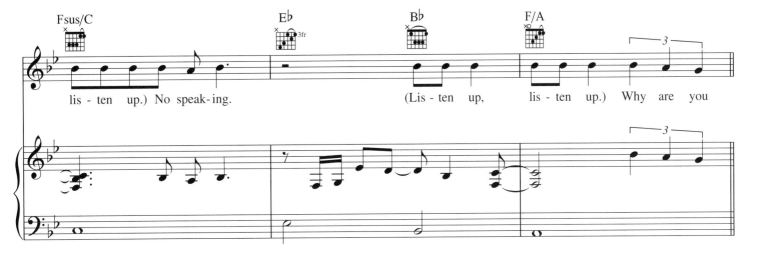

lis - ten up.) No speak - ing. (Lis - ten up, lis - ten up.) Why are you

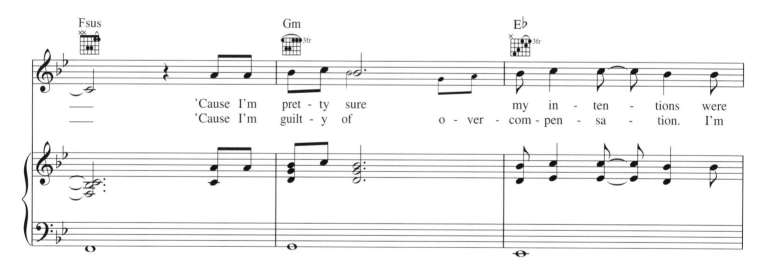

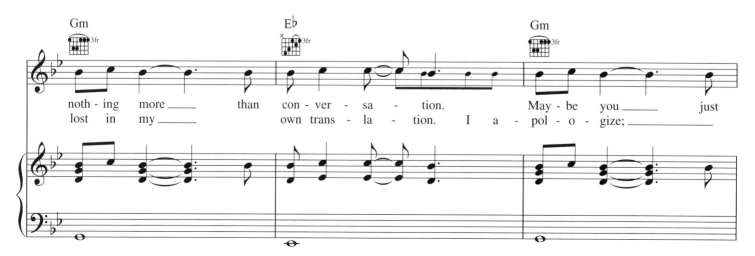

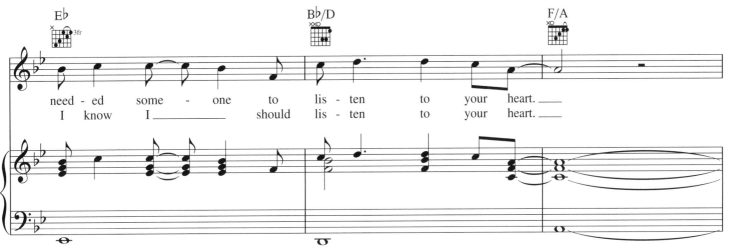

need - ed some - one to lis - ten to your heart. ____
I know I ____ should lis - ten to your heart. ____

May - be I spoke ____ too soon, ____ may - be I said ____ too much. ____

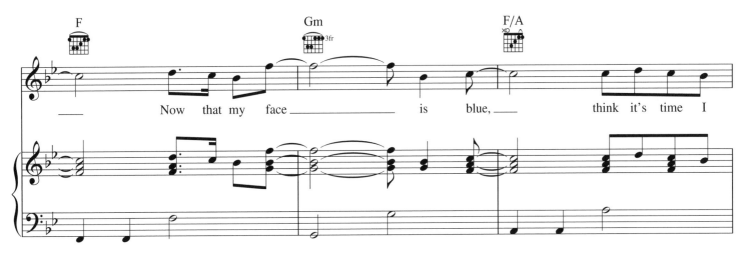

____ Now that my face ____ is blue, ____ think it's time I

lis - ten up. ____
(1.,2.) I've al - read - y said e - nough. ____
(3.) Think it's time I

(Lis - ten up, lis - ten up. Lis - ten up,

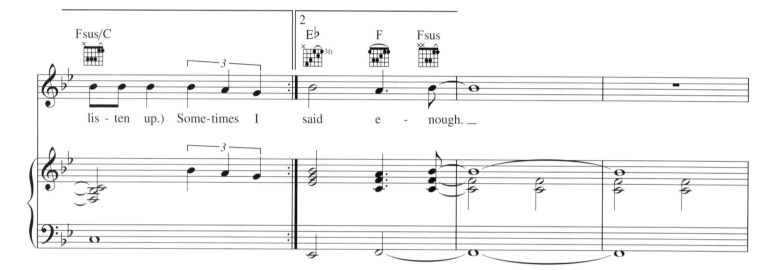

lis - ten up.) Some - times I said e - nough.

There is - n't an - y - thing that I could say, __ not a word __ to

get in the way __ of you, __ of __ you. __ I am lis -

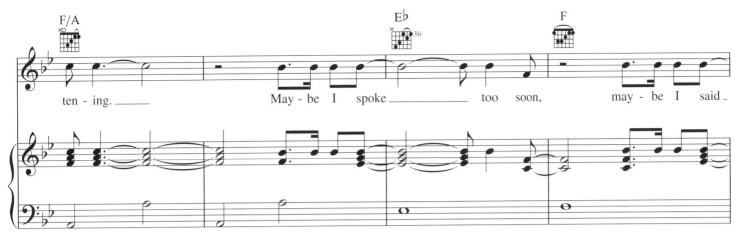

ten - ing. _____ May - be I spoke _____ too soon, may - be I said _

_____ too much. _____ Now that my face _____ is blue, _

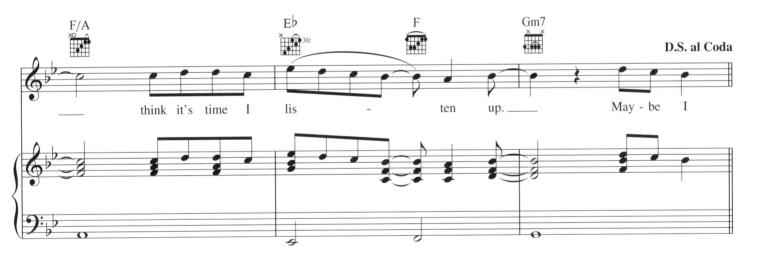

D.S. al Coda

_____ think it's time I lis - ten up. _____ May - be I

CODA

lis - ten up. _____ I've al - read - y said e - nough. _

FIGHT ANOTHER DAY

Words and Music by BRANDON HEATH,
DANIEL MUCKALA and JESS CATES

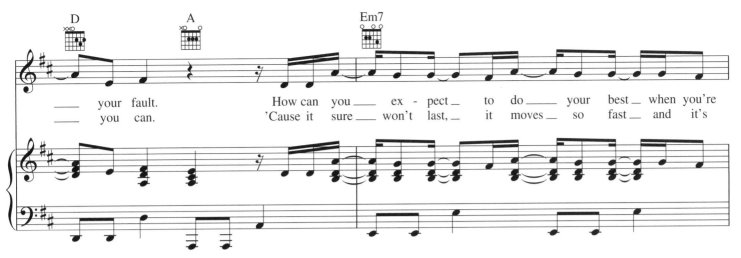

your fault. How can you ___ ex - pect ___ to do ___ your best ___ when you're
you can. 'Cause it sure ___ won't last, ___ it moves ___ so fast ___ and it's

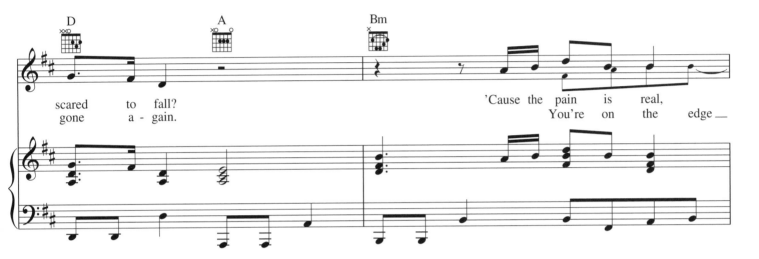

scared   to fall? 'Cause the pain   is   real,
gone   a - gain. You're   on   the   edge ___

___ but you will sur - vive. ___ That's how you know you're a - live. ___
now, ___ but you will sur - vive. ___ That's how you know you're a - live. ___

'Cause } it's o - kay   now,   hey   now,
And }

you can let go. ____ That's when you find out, find out that

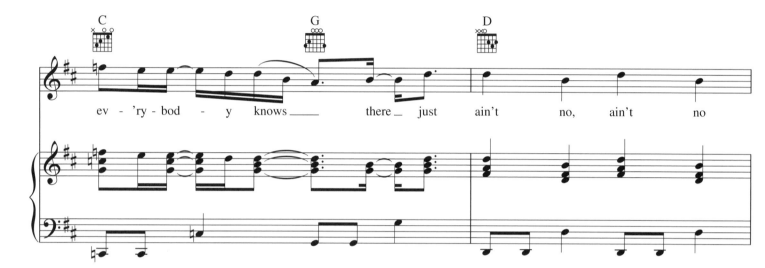

ev - 'ry - bod - y knows ____ there ____ just ain't no, ain't no

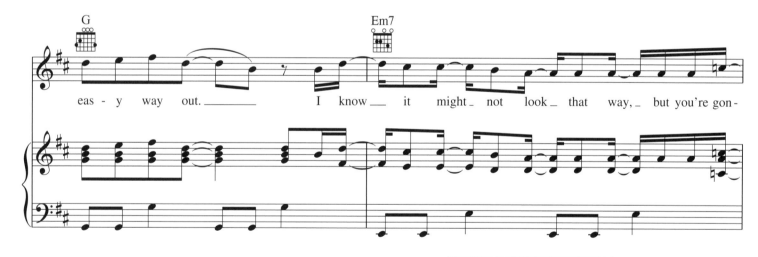

eas - y way out. ____ I know ____ it might ____ not look ____ that way, ____ but you're gon-

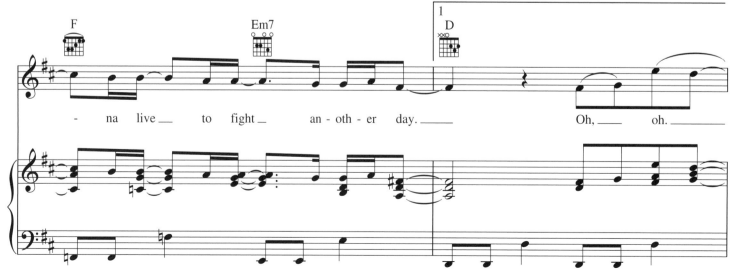

- na live ____ to fight ____ an - oth - er day. ____ Oh, ____ oh. _____

Oh, __ oh. _____ Oh, __ oh. _____ There's a place __

An-oth-er day, __ yeah. __ You won-der what you are made __

__ of. I'm tell - ing you now, _____ you're gon - na make __

__ it some - how. What are you so a - fraid __ of? ___

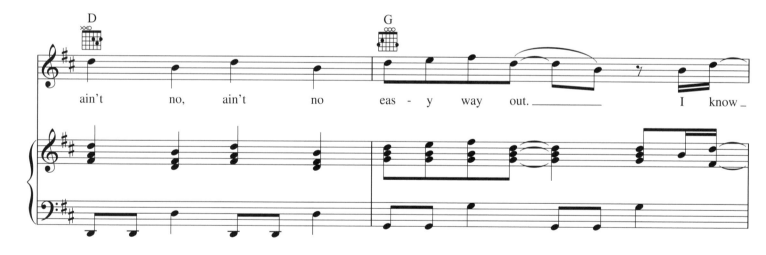

WHEN I'M ALONE

Words and Music by BRANDON HEATH
and NATE CAMPANY

This is my dream and my gift, ___ but some-times I get
The depth of the things that I've missed, ___ they leave me like this:

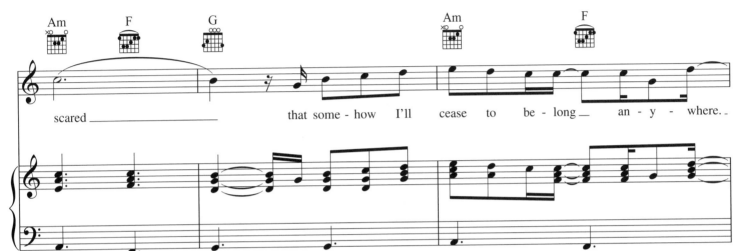

scared _____ that some - how I'll cease to be - long ___ an - y - where. ___

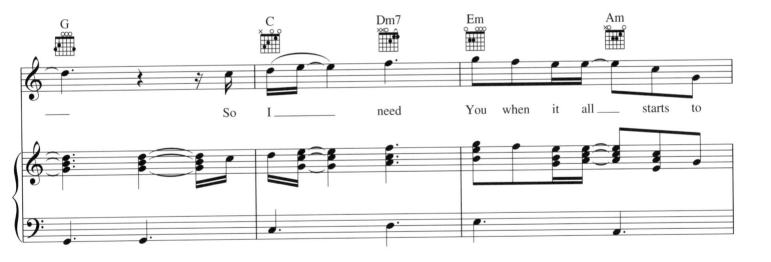

So I _____ need You when it all ___ starts to

show, when I'm a - lone. ___

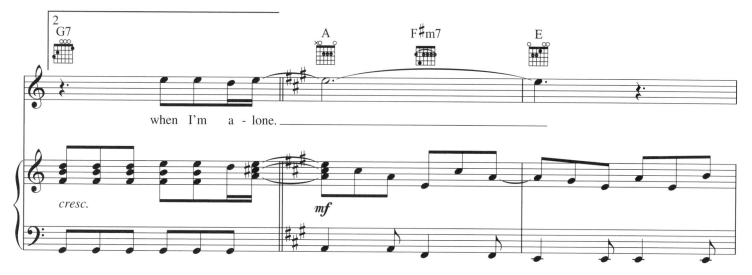

when I'm a - lone. _____

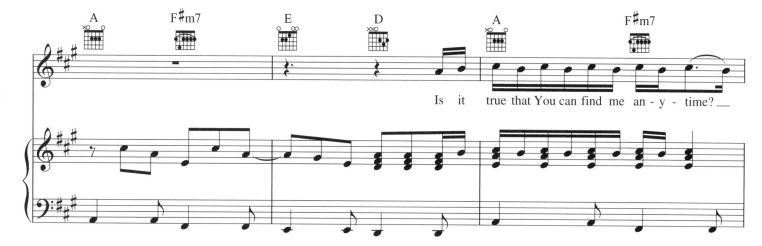

Is it true that You can find me an - y - time? __

'Cause I'm feel - ing like I'm there; it's a -

bout that time. __ 'Cause I'm scared _____ that some - how I'll

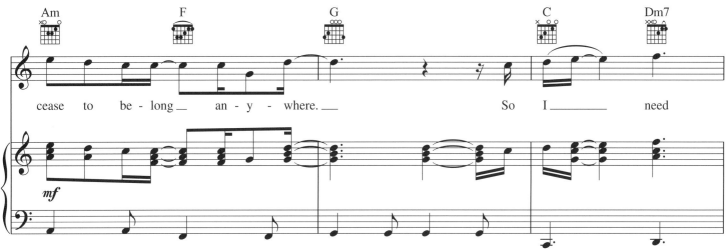

cease to be-long ___ an-y-where. ___ So I _____ need

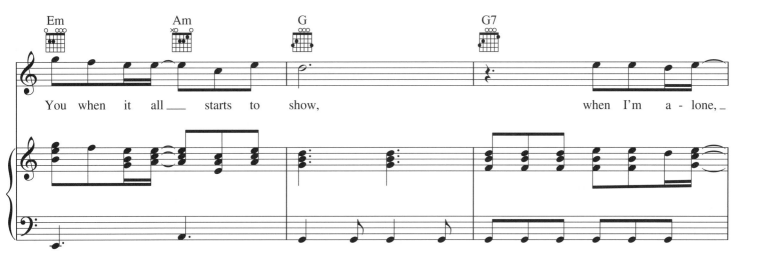

You when it all ___ starts to show, when I'm a-lone, ___

when I'm a-lone, _____

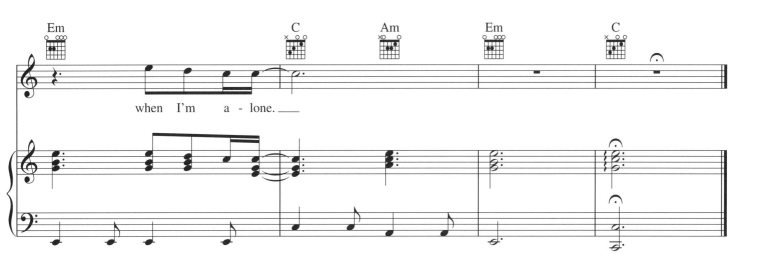

when I'm a-lone. ___

NO NOT ONE

Words and Music by CHRISTY NOCKELS
and BRANDON HEATH

No bet-ter ___ word ___

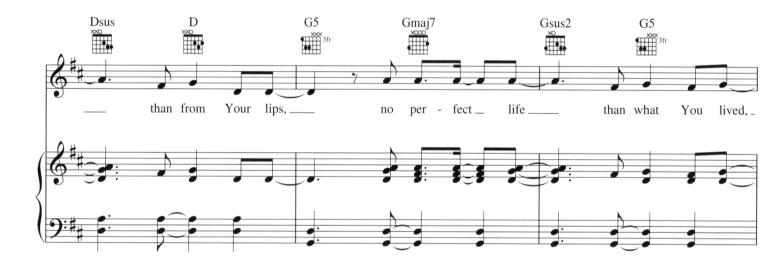

___ than from Your lips, ___ no per-fect ___ life ___ than what You lived, ___

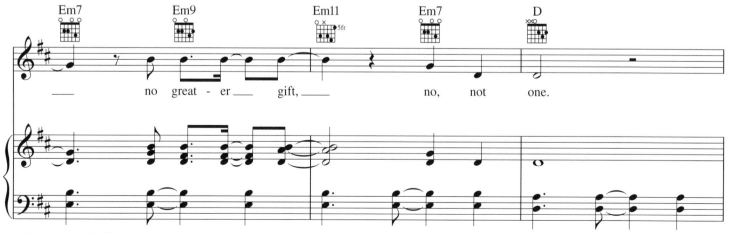

___ no great-er ___ gift, ___ no, not one.

* Recorded a half step lower.

No bright - er _____ star _____
No im - age _____ true _____

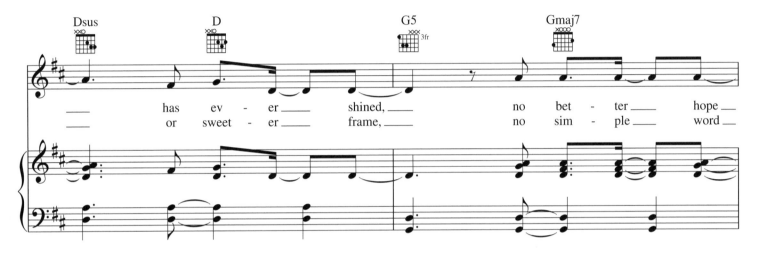

_____ has ev - er _____ shined, _____ no bet - ter _____ hope _____
_____ or sweet - er _____ frame, _____ no sim - ple _____ word _____

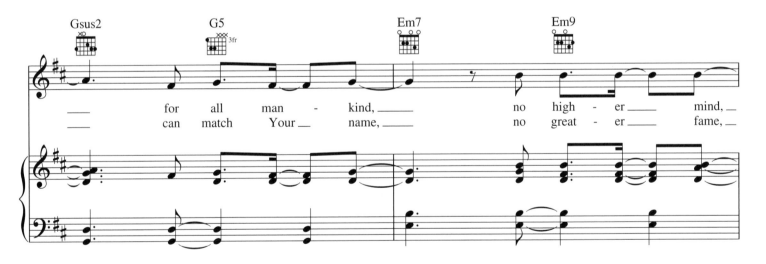

_____ for all man - kind, _____ no high - er _____ mind, _
_____ can match Your _ name, _____ no great - er _____ fame, _

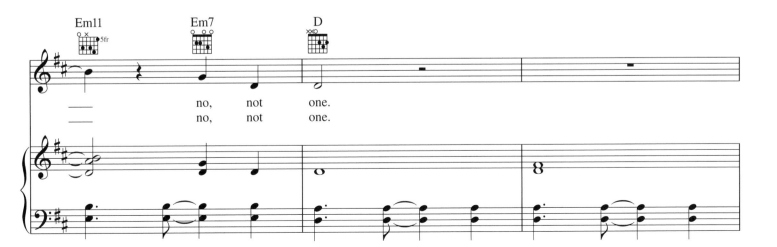

_____ no, not one.
_____ no, not one.

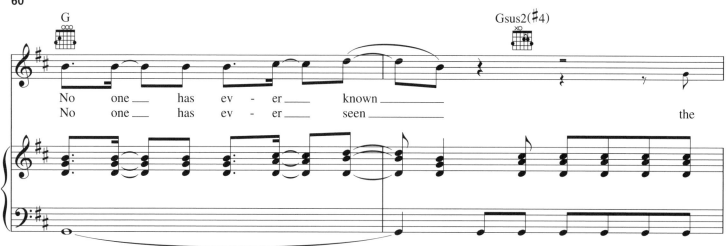

No one ___ has ev - er ___ known _____
No one ___ has ev - er ___ seen _____ the

this kind ___ of love You've ___ shown. _____ There has nev -
depth of ___ Your maj - es - ty. _____

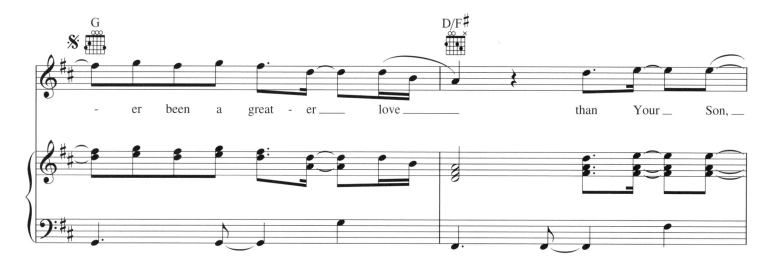

- er been a great - er ___ love _____ than Your ___ Son, ___

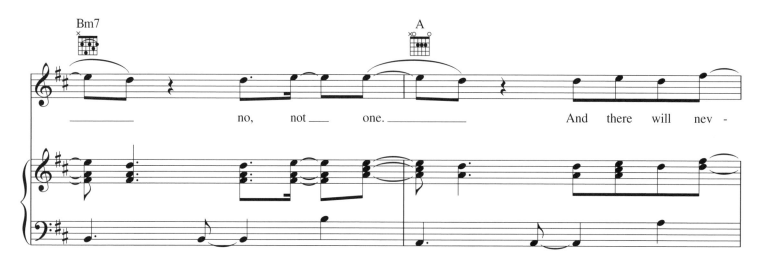

_____ no, not ___ one. _____ And there will nev -

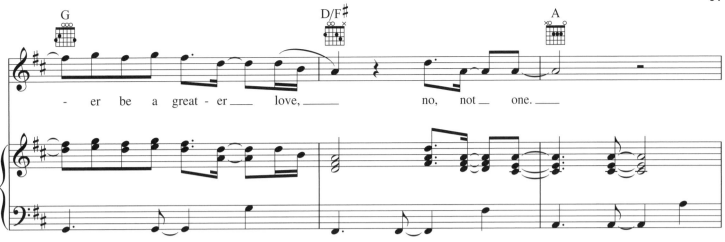

-er be a great-er ___ love, ___ no, not ___ one. ___

With His life, ___ You have for-giv-en ___ us. ___ Hope has ___ come, ___

___ hope has ___ come, ___ and there will nev - er be a great-er ___ love, ___

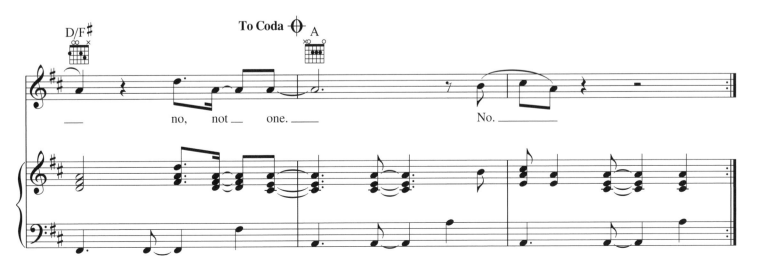

___ no, not ___ one. ___ No. ___

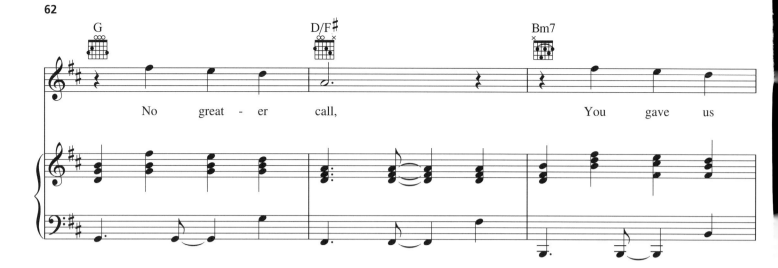

No great-er call, You gave us

all a rea-son to live.___ No great-er love,

You gave us all a rea-son to give.___ No great-er

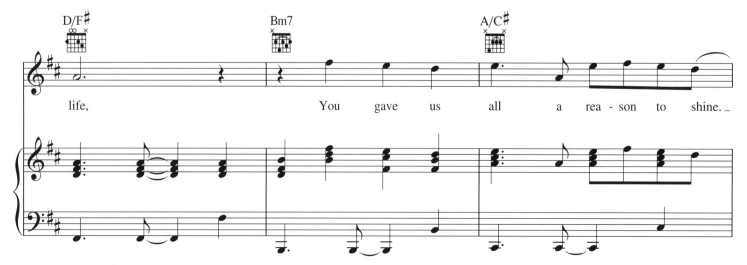

life, You gave us all a rea-son to shine.__

No great-er love, for-ev-er____ mine.____

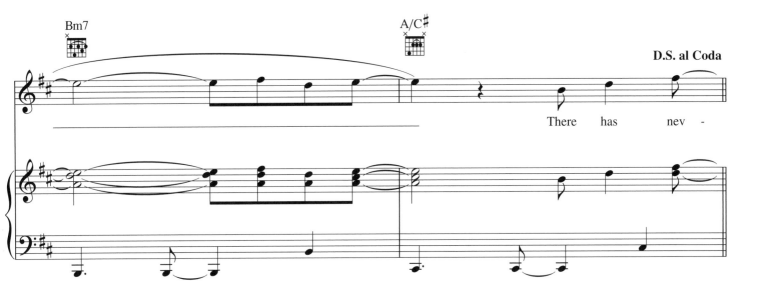

D.S. al Coda

There has nev-

CODA

More Contemporary Christian Folios from Hal Leonard
Arranged for Piano, Voice and Guitar

AVALON – THE GREATEST HITS

This best-of collection showcases 15 signature songs from throughout their career, plus a brand new tune soon to be fan favorite, the radio hit "Still My God." Includes: Adonai • Can't Live a Day • New Day • You Were There • and more.

00307056 P/V/G..................................$17.99

JEREMY CAMP – SPEAKING LOUDER THAN BEFORE

Our matching folio to the latest from this three-time ASCAP Songwriter of the Year includes the hit "There Will Be a Day" and 11 more: Capture Me • I'm Alive • My Fortress • Surrender • You Will Be There • and more.

00307031 P/V/G.......................................$16.99

CASTING CROWNS – UNTIL THE WHOLE WORLD HEARS

Matching folio to the 2009 release featuring 11 songs from this Christian pop group: Always Enough • Joyful, Joyful • At Your Feet • Holy One • To Know You • Mercy • Blessed Redeemer • and more.

00307107 P/V/G..................................$16.99

STEVEN CURTIS CHAPMAN – BEAUTY WILL RISE

Matching folio to Chapman's touching release that was written in response to the death of one of his daughters. 12 songs, including: Just Have to Wait • Faithful • Heaven Is the Face • I Will Trust You • and more.

00307100 P/V/G..................................$16.99

DAVID CROWDER*BAND – CHURCH MUSIC

Our matching folio to the innovative 2009 release features 17 tunes, including the hit single "How He Loves" and: All Around Me • Can I Lie Here • Oh, Happiness • Shadows • We Are Loved • What a Miracle • and more.

00307089 P/V/G..................................$17.99

AMY GRANT – GREATEST HITS

This collection assembles 19 of her finest, including: Angels • Baby Baby • El Shaddai • Father's Eyes • Good for Me • Lead Me On • Simple Things • Stay for Awhile • and more.
00306948 P/V/G $17.95

Prices, contents, and availability subject to change without notice.

HEATHER HEADLEY – AUDIENCE OF ONE

Features 10 songs or medleys of well-known gospel standards plus some Headley originals and other recent favorites: Here I Am to Worship • I Know the Lord Will Make a Way • Simply Redeemed • Zion • and more.

00307057 Piano/Vocal..........................$16.99

KUTLESS – IT IS WELL

Matching folio to the second worship album from these Christian rockers, featuring 12 songs, including: Give Us Clean Hands • God of Wonders • Redeemer • What Faith Can Do • and more.
00307099 P/V/G $16.99

MARY MARY – THE SOUND

Features vocal arrangements with piano accompaniment for all 11 songs off the Gospel chart-topping 5th CD from this R&B/gospel duo. Includes the Grammy-winning single "Get Up" and: Boom • Dirt • Forgiven Me • God in Me • I Worship You • and more.

00307039 Piano/Vocal..........................$16.99

RECOLLECTION: THE BEST OF NICHOLE NORDEMAN

This 17-song collection features the finest releases from this popular CCM singer/songwriter, plus two new songs – "Sunrise" and "Finally Free." Includes: Brave • Fool for You • Real to Me • River God • This Mystery • and more.

00306633 P/V/G..................................$17.95

PHILLIPS, CRAIG & DEAN – THE ULTIMATE COLLECTION

31 songs spanning the career of this popular CCM trio: Favorite Song of All • Hallelujah (Your Love Is Amazing) • I Want to Be Just like You • Shine on Us • Your Grace Still Amazes Me • and more.

00306789 P/V/G..................................$19.95

THE BEST OF MATT REDMAN

14 modern worship songs, including: Beautiful News • Better Is One Day • Blessed Be Your Name • The Heart of Worship • Once Again • Shine • Undignified • You Never Let Go • and more.

00307080 P/V/G..................................$16.99

SANCTUS REAL – WE NEED EACH OTHER

The fourth CD from this Dove Award-winning Toledo quintet features 10 songs: Half Our Lives • Leap of Faith • Legacy • Sing • Turn On the Lights • We Need Each Other • Whatever You're Doing (Something Heavenly) • and more.

00306976 P/V/G..................................$16.95

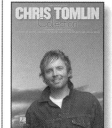

SWITCHFOOT – THE BEST YET

This greatest hits compilation features the newly released song "This Is Home" and 17 other top songs. Includes: Concrete Girl • Dare You to Move • Learning to Breathe • Meant to Live • Only Hope • Stars • and more.
00307030 P/V/G $17.99

THIRD DAY – REVELATION

All 13 songs from the chart-topping album, including the #1 single "Call My Name" and: Born Again • I Will Always Be True • Let Me Love You • Run to You • Slow Down • Take It All • and more.

00307005 P/V/G..................................$16.95

THE CHRIS TOMLIN COLLECTION

15 songs from one of the leading artists and composers in contemporary worship music, including the favorites: Amazing Grace (My Chains Are Gone) • Indescribable • We Fall Down • and more.

00306951P/V/G..................................$16.95

THE BEST OF CECE WINANS

14 favorite songs from the gospel superstar: Alabaster Box • He's Always There • It Wasn't Easy • Looking Back at You • Pray • Purified • Throne Room • What About You • and more.

00306912P/V/G..................................$16.99